A DINOSAUR Q&A BOOK

WOULD A DINOSAUR EAT MY TEACHER?

Photo credits:

Louis Chiappe—p. 25
Howard S. Friedman—p. 6
François Gohier—pp. 13, 18, 21
The Granger Collection—p. 18
John Gurche—p. 8
Breck Kent—p. 26
Nicolas Le Corre—p. 28
Carl Mehling—p. 25
National Academy of Natural Sciences,
  Philadelphia—p. 8
Natural History Museum, London—pp. 7, 9, 10,
  12, 15, 17, 20, 24, 28, 29; Orbis: pp. 19, 21, 22;
  J. Sibbick: cover, pp. 2–3, 14, 16, 17, 30–31;
  Maurice Wilson: p. 27
Peabody Museum of Natural History, Yale
  University—p. 11
Toho, Ltd.—p. 19
Eric Vandeville—p. 22

Illustration credits:

Paul Michalak—cover, p. 6
Justin Ray Thompson—all other illustrations

Visit us at *www.kidsbooks.com*.
Volume discounts available for group purchases.

A DINOSAUR Q&A BOOK

WOULD A DINOSAUR EAT MY TEACHER?

By
Carl Mehling
American Museum
of Natural History

kidsbooks
Incorporated

A. That would depend on whether it was a carnivore (meat-eater) or a herbivore (plant-eater). The biggest dinosaurs that ever lived would have left your teacher alone because they were herbivores. Take *Brachiosaurus* (BRAK-ee-uh-SORE-us) *(below, right)*, for example. It was about 13 feet tall at the hips, 90 feet long, and 25 tons, but ate only plants. On the other hand, *Deinonychus* (dye-NON-ih-kus) *(below, left)* was only about 13 feet long, 5 feet tall, and 175 pounds, but it would have been happy to chow down on your teacher—and on you, too!

Q. What kind of salad did Mesozoic dinosaurs eat?

A. Many kinds of plants that still live today also existed in the Mesozoic Era—the time when the giant dinosaurs lived. Giant herbivores may have eaten ferns and horsetails, which are small plants found in wet areas. They also may have eaten ginkgoes, palms, or oaks, all of which are leafy trees familiar to us now. They also may have added a fruity dessert to their menu: Grapes and figs were around back then as well.

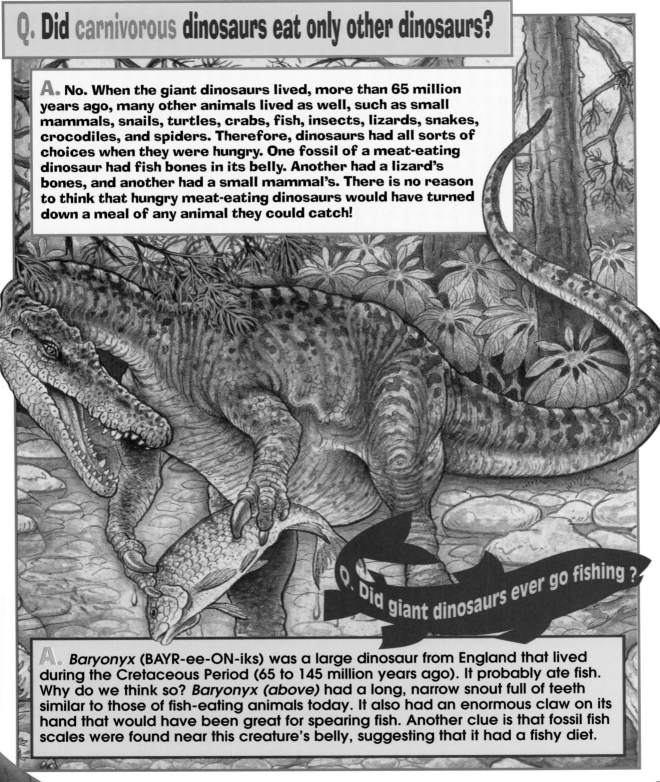

Q. Did carnivorous dinosaurs eat only other dinosaurs?

A. No. When the giant dinosaurs lived, more than 65 million years ago, many other animals lived as well, such as small mammals, snails, turtles, crabs, fish, insects, lizards, snakes, crocodiles, and spiders. Therefore, dinosaurs had all sorts of choices when they were hungry. One fossil of a meat-eating dinosaur had fish bones in its belly. Another had a lizard's bones, and another had a small mammal's. There is no reason to think that hungry meat-eating dinosaurs would have turned down a meal of any animal they could catch!

Q. Did giant dinosaurs ever go fishing?

A. *Baryonyx* (BAYR-ee-ON-iks) was a large dinosaur from England that lived during the Cretaceous Period (65 to 145 million years ago). It probably ate fish. Why do we think so? *Baryonyx (above)* had a long, narrow snout full of teeth similar to those of fish-eating animals today. It also had an enormous claw on its hand that would have been great for spearing fish. Another clue is that fossil fish scales were found near this creature's belly, suggesting that it had a fishy diet.

Q. Is this a book about Pachypoda?

A. Yes. Pachypoda (pak-ee-POE-duh), which means "thick foot," was the first term used to describe the group of animals that we now call dinosaurs. The word *Pachypoda* was introduced in 1836 by scientist Hermann von Meyer. At that time, however, there was little public interest in

these animals. It was not until 1842, when information about how remarkable these animals were started to circulate, that people became interested in them. By then, another scientist, Sir Richard Owen, had used the term *dinosaur*, meaning "fearfully great lizard," to describe these prehistoric animals (such as the Barosaurus at right)—and that is the name that stuck.

Q. What fossil dinosaur was the first to walk through a museum?

A. *Hadrosaurus foulkii* (HAD-ruh-SORE-us FULL-key-eye). When this dinosaur *(at right)* was unearthed in New Jersey in 1858, it was the first skeleton found with enough bones to show what giant dinosaurs looked like. Ten years later, a mounted specimen was created from those bones and displayed at the Academy of Natural Sciences in Philadelphia. This was the first mounted fossil dinosaur that the public had ever seen. Giant dinosaurs quickly became a museum favorite all over the world.

Q. How did we find out what the names of prehistoric dinosaurs were?

A. Humans invented them. Fossil dinosaurs are named for characteristics of their bones or for unique qualities they have. They are also named after people, places, imaginary monsters, or just about anything else. *Gasosaurus (right)* was so named because it was discovered by workers from a gas company. If you got the chance to name a dinosaur, how would you create its name?

Q. When is a "saurus" not a dinosaur?

A. Dinosaurs are not lizards, but early fossil finders thought that they were. That is why many dinosaur names end with the suffix –*saurus*, a Greek word meaning "lizard." However, not every name ending in –*saurus* belongs to a dinosaur. For instance, *Elasmosaurus (above)* was a reptile that lived in the sea; *Mastodonsaurus* was a huge early amphibian. Many fossil reptiles, such as *Mosasaurus* and *Thoracosaurus*, were not dinosaurs. Some modern reptiles have names ending in –*saurus*, such as *Xenosaurus*. You can also find a thesaurus, which is not even an animal—it's a book! (In that case, the –*saurus* came from a Latin word meaning "collection" or "treasure.")

Q. True or false?

All dinosaur fossils begin to form when the animal dies.

A. False. Animals don't have to sit around waiting for death before they can make their mark on the fossil record. Things like eggs (*below*) and footprints (*in the background*) can become fossils. Think about how many eggs and footprints one dinosaur can make in its lifetime—thousands! Also, many dinosaurs broke off teeth while chomping on hard things, like bones. All those lost teeth can start becoming fossils long before the animal dies.

Q. Has a dinosaur ever put its foot in its mouth?

A. Probably not. But a rare fossil found in what is now the Walter Kidde Dinosaur Park in New Jersey comes close to that description. Fossil dinosaur bones are almost never found where fossil dinosaur tracks are found. In northern New Jersey, however, a footprint was found with a dinosaur tooth in it. The trackmaker, which was a large Early Jurassic carnivore, had squished its foot into the mud, leaving a footprint. A tooth from a meat-eating dinosaur was found in that footprint. Did the tooth belong to the trackmaker or to a different dinosaur? Nobody knows.

Q. *Eubrontes* is the official state fossil of which U.S. state?

A. Connecticut. However, *Eubrontes* (yoo-BRON-teez) isn't the name of a dinosaur—it is the name of the fossil footprints of a dinosaur! Scientists give fossil tracks and footprints special names that are different from the names given to skeletons. This is because we may never know which animal made a set of tracks unless it died at the end of its tracks and became a fossil along with them. *Eubrontes* tracks *(above)*—which belong to an early, large, carnivorous dinosaur—are common in Connecticut, but no bones of the likely trackmaker have ever been found.

Q. Where did dinosaurs leave the tiniest fossil footprints?

A. The smallest known fossil dinosaur footprints were found near Parrsboro, Nova Scotia, Canada, by a man named Eldon George. George was fossil hunting along the cliffs of the Bay of Fundy when he found a block of stone with many tiny footprints on it. These tracks came from a very early meat-eating dinosaur. Each track was only an inch long. This mini-monster, which was just a baby, was such a peewee that it would have fit in your hands.

Q. WHICH DINOSAUR THUMBED ITS NOSE AT ITS DISCOVERERS?

A. When *Iguanodon* (ih-GWAHN-uh-don) was discovered in the early 1800s, only partial skeletons were found. Scientists had no idea what the giant dinosaurs had looked like, so they guessed. They had found a spikelike bone with the remains. Since they thought *Iguanodon* was much like a giant iguana and, since some modern iguanas have small nose horns, they put the spiky bone on this new animal's nose *(below)*. Years later, complete skeletons were found. They showed that what scientists thought was a "nose horn" was actually *Iguanodon*'s thumb bone *(left)*!

RIGHT

WRONG

Q. Can dinosaur fossils be found at the bottom of the ocean?

A. Maybe. In 1916, a ship called *Mount Temple* sailed for England with a load of fossil dinosaur bones collected by the famous North American dinosaur hunter, Charles H. Sternberg. On board were two skeletons of duckbill dinosaurs—one of which Sternberg considered to be one of the finest fossils he ever collected. Unfortunately, the ship sank in the Atlantic. Some scientists think that the bones dissolved, but others believe that a dinosaur coffin lies at the bottom of the sea.

Q. What early dinosaur was a party animal?

A. A very early dinosaur was recently discovered in Brazil. The incomplete skeletons of three animals were found showing that this dinosaur had been a small herbivore, about five feet long. It belongs to the group of dinosaurs called sauropodomorpha (SAWR-uh-pod-uh-MOR-fuh), which means "lizard-foot form." The new dinosaur was named *Saturnalia* (SAT-ur-NAIL-yuh). That name was chosen because two of the specimens were found during a Brazilian festival called Saturnalia, which is a time of feasting and partying.

Q. Did dinosaurs ever collect fossils?

A. Sort of. The largest land animals that ever lived were the sauropods—plant–eating dinosaurs with long necks. They didn't chew their food. Instead, they swallowed bunches of plants whole. To grind up this plant matter, the sauropods swallowed stones, which they moved around in a muscular pouch called a gizzard. These stones, called gastroliths (GAS–troh–liths), are sometimes found with giant fossil skeletons. Occasionally, the gastroliths contain small fossils of things, such as coral, that are millions of years older than the dinosaur that "collected" them!

Q. Which Mesozoic dinosaurs could have played in the snow?

A. Most Mesozoic dinosaurs lived in places that probably did not get snow. But some found in Australia probably did get to play in the snow! During the Late Cretaceous, Australia was closer to the South Pole than it is today. When winter began, many dinosaurs migrated long distances to warmer weather. But some dinosaurs, called hypsilophodonts (HIP-suh-LOH-fuh-donts), were too small to migrate, so they spent the cold winters at home—and probably had lots of snow.

Q. Which dinosaur would win a popularity contest?

A. *Tyrannosaurus rex (above).* Anyone who knows anything about dinosaurs has heard of *T. rex*, which may be the world's best-known dinosaur. Playing a major role in movies, especially the mega-hit *Jurassic Park*, hasn't hurt the status of this carnivore, either. At 40 feet long and 15 feet tall (you wouldn't even have reached its knee), *T. rex* was one of the biggest meat-eaters ever to walk on Earth. You can tell that *T. rex* is popular: It's the only dinosaur that goes by its nickname.

Q. WHICH DINOSAUR RULED WITH AN ?

A. *Astrodon* (AST-roh-don) *(below)* is the largest Early Cretaceous dinosaur from the eastern part of North America. *Astrodon* is also the official state dinosaur of Maryland. *Astrodon* rules! This sauropod (long-necked, plant-eating dino) had arms that were longer than its legs, making it a brachiosaur (BRAK-ee-uh-sore). The bones of *Astrodon* were exposed in the 1800s when iron ore miners dug up huge amounts of rock. If the miners hadn't found *Astrodon*, it might have remained buried forever.

Q. Which dinosaur could be called a living fortress?

A. *Animantarx* (an-uh-MAN-tarks). It was a medium-sized (9-10 feet long) ankylosaur that lived during the Early Cretaceous Period in what is now Utah, U.S. Ankylosaurs were heavily armored herbivores that are sometimes called living tanks. *Animantarx* was a nodosaur, a kind of ankylosaur that lacked a bony tail club. However, it did have armor all over its body and small horns on its cheeks and above its eyes. That is why this animal—named in 1999—was called *Animantarx*, which means "living fortress."

15

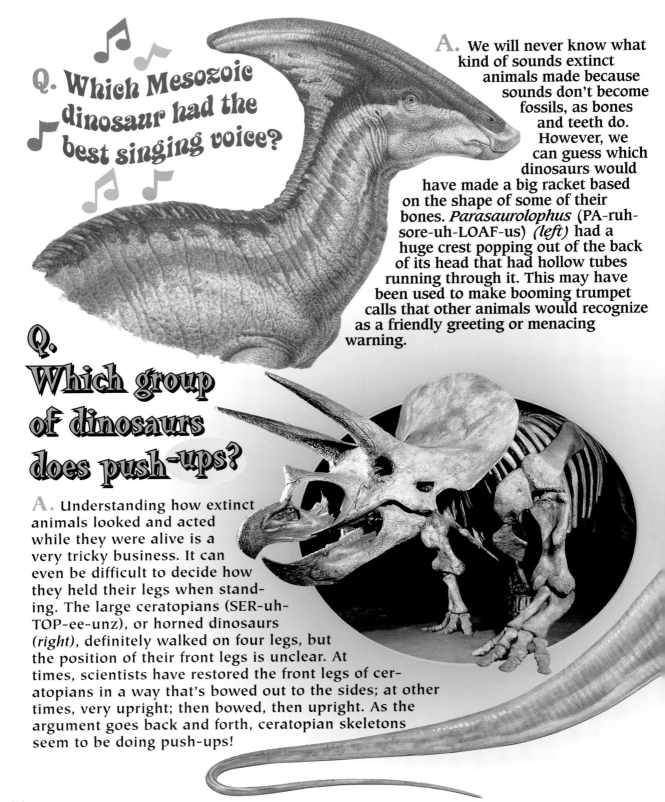

Q. Which Mesozoic dinosaur had the best singing voice?

A. We will never know what kind of sounds extinct animals made because sounds don't become fossils, as bones and teeth do. However, we can guess which dinosaurs would have made a big racket based on the shape of some of their bones. *Parasaurolophus* (PA-ruh-sore-uh-LOAF-us) *(left)* had a huge crest popping out of the back of its head that had hollow tubes running through it. This may have been used to make booming trumpet calls that other animals would recognize as a friendly greeting or menacing warning.

Q. Which group of dinosaurs does push-ups?

A. Understanding how extinct animals looked and acted while they were alive is a very tricky business. It can even be difficult to decide how they held their legs when standing. The large ceratopians (SER-uh-TOP-ee-unz), or horned dinosaurs *(right)*, definitely walked on four legs, but the position of their front legs is unclear. At times, scientists have restored the front legs of ceratopians in a way that's bowed out to the sides; at other times, very upright; then bowed, then upright. As the argument goes back and forth, ceratopian skeletons seem to be doing push-ups!

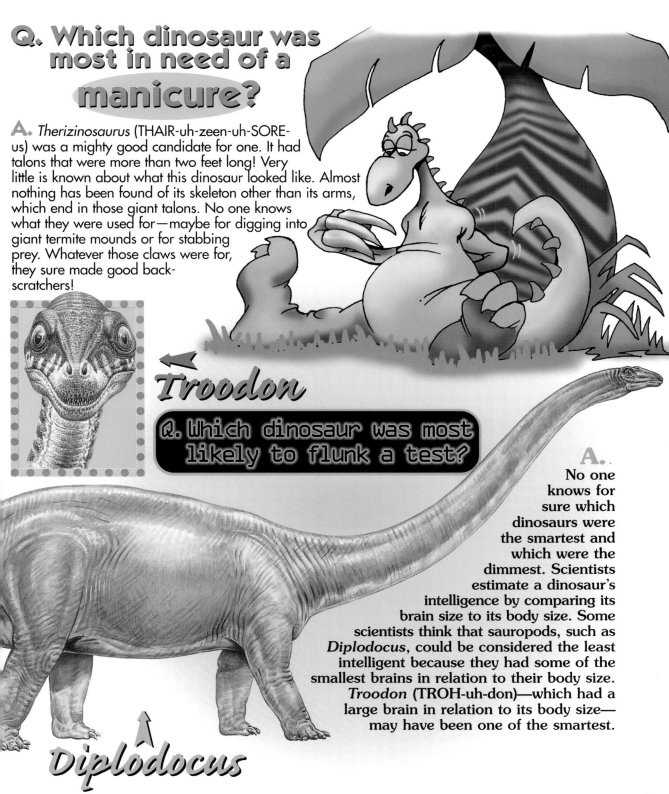

Q. Which dinosaur was most in need of a manicure?

A. *Therizinosaurus* (THAIR-uh-zeen-uh-SORE-us) was a mighty good candidate for one. It had talons that were more than two feet long! Very little is known about what this dinosaur looked like. Almost nothing has been found of its skeleton other than its arms, which end in those giant talons. No one knows what they were used for—maybe for digging into giant termite mounds or for stabbing prey. Whatever those claws were for, they sure made good back-scratchers!

Troodon

Q. Which dinosaur was most likely to flunk a test?

A. No one knows for sure which dinosaurs were the smartest and which were the dimmest. Scientists estimate a dinosaur's intelligence by comparing its brain size to its body size. Some scientists think that sauropods, such as *Diplodocus*, could be considered the least intelligent because they had some of the smallest brains in relation to their body size. *Troodon* (TROH-uh-don)—which had a large brain in relation to its body size— may have been one of the smartest.

Diplodocus

Q. Were griffins really prehistoric dinosaurs?

A. The griffin is a mythical animal that is part eagle and part lion. In many stories about the griffin, it sounds a lot like *Protoceratops* (Pro-toh-SAIR-uh-tops). *Protoceratops (right)* was a Cretaceous dinosaur found in Mongolia. It had a beak that looks very much like the beak shown in ancient drawings of the griffin. *Protoceratops* fossils are common in the area where ancient Asians hunted for gold. Perhaps these early traders imagined griffins to be gold-guarding creatures—and told scary griffin stories so their gold mines would be left alone.

Q. Which dinosaur might have met the Jabberwock?

A. *Borogovia* (bor-uh-GO-vee-uh), named in 1987, was a small carnivore found in Mongolia. It was named for an imaginary animal that appears in the poem "Jabberwocky," from the book *Through the Looking Glass* by Lewis Carroll. The main character, Alice, hears a fanciful story about a monster called the Jabberwock *(above)* that lives in a land with creatures called borogoves. Borogoves are described as thin, shabby-looking birds with feathers sticking out all around—something like a live mop. *Borogovia* probably had feathers, too, although it would be hard to say whether they were shabby-looking or not.

Q. Did a dinosaur ever fight with Hercules?

A. Sort of. Achelous (uh-KEE-lus) was a shape-changing, river god in Greek and Roman mythology. He transformed himself into a bull to fight Hercules, but was defeated when Hercules tore off one of his horns. *Achelousaurus* (uh-KEE-luh-SORE-us), named in 1995, was a large Cretaceous "horned" dinosaur with horns on its head, but not its face. Since *Achelousaurus* appears to be a kind of shape changer, having the features of several related dinosaurs, who "lost" its horns, it carries the name of Hercules' enemy Achelous.

Q. Was Godzilla a dinosaur?

A. No. Godzilla was a movie monster that was entirely made up. But, in 1997, a new, 200 million-year-old fossil dinosaur was found in New Mexico and named *Gojirasaurus* (go-JEE-ruh-SAW-rus), which means "Godzilla lizard." Most dinosaurs from this time were kind of small, but the *Gojirasaurus* fossil shows an animal over 18 feet long—and it was not fully grown. This would make *Gojirasaurus* the "monster" of its time.

Q. How do you tell boy dinosaurs from girl dinosaurs in fossils?

A. That is hard to do, but there are a couple of hints. Sometimes, many skeletons of one kind of dinosaur are found. If there seem to be two different "styles" of that animal, one is probably male and the other female, though you can't say which is which. Also, some dinosaur fossils are preserved with tailbones called chevrons. Modern crocodile chevrons differ in number and shape for males and females; the same may be true for dinosaurs.

Q. Did baby dinosaurs ever drink milk?

A. Probably not. The only animals that feed milk to their babies are mammals, such as mice, whales, bats, deer, and humans. Birds do not feed milk to their babies, nor do crocodiles. Dinosaurs have no close relationship to mammals, so it is unlikely that dinosaurs, such as the Maiasaurus at right, fed their babies milk.

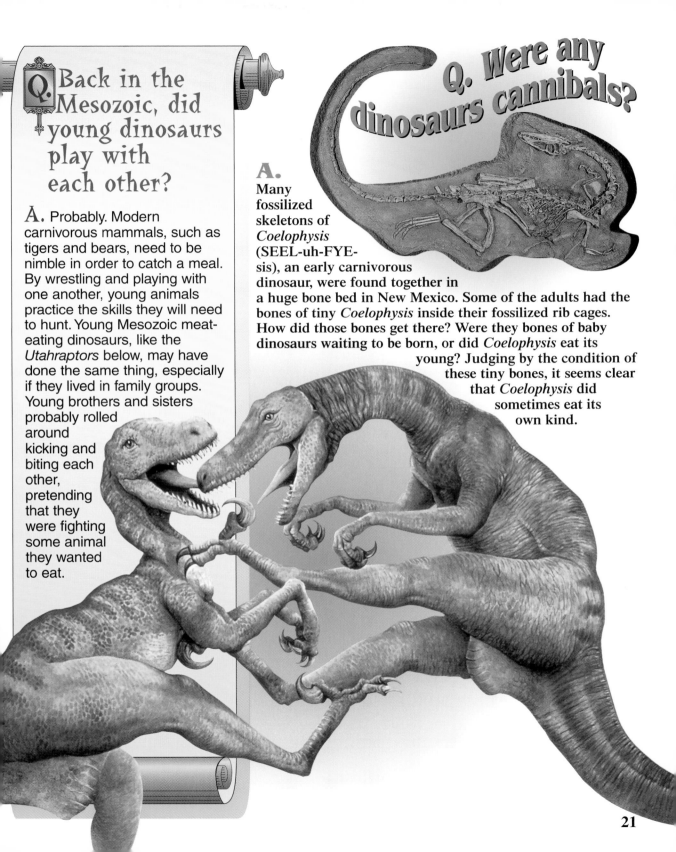

A. Probably. Modern carnivorous mammals, such as tigers and bears, need to be nimble in order to catch a meal. By wrestling and playing with one another, young animals practice the skills they will need to hunt. Young Mesozoic meat-eating dinosaurs, like the *Utahraptors* below, may have done the same thing, especially if they lived in family groups. Young brothers and sisters probably rolled around kicking and biting each other, pretending that they were fighting some animal they wanted to eat.

A. Many fossilized skeletons of *Coelophysis* (SEEL-uh-FYE-sis), an early carnivorous dinosaur, were found together in a huge bone bed in New Mexico. Some of the adults had the bones of tiny *Coelophysis* inside their fossilized rib cages. How did those bones get there? Were they bones of baby dinosaurs waiting to be born, or did *Coelophysis* eat its young? Judging by the condition of these tiny bones, it seems clear that *Coelophysis* did sometimes eat its own kind.

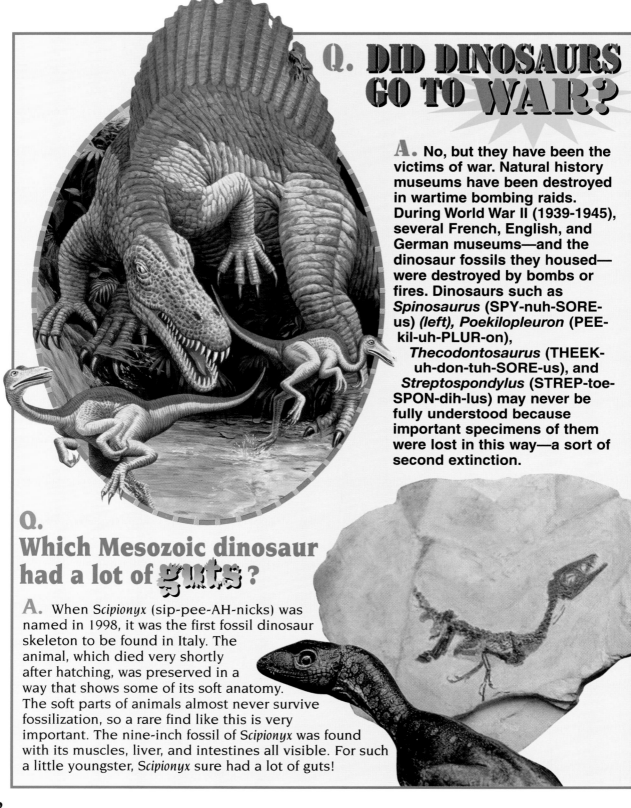

Q. DID DINOSAURS GO TO WAR?

A. No, but they have been the victims of war. Natural history museums have been destroyed in wartime bombing raids. During World War II (1939-1945), several French, English, and German museums—and the dinosaur fossils they housed—were destroyed by bombs or fires. Dinosaurs such as *Spinosaurus* (SPY-nuh-SORE-us) *(left)*, *Poekilopleuron* (PEE-kil-uh-PLUR-on), *Thecodontosaurus* (THEEK-uh-don-tuh-SORE-us), and *Streptospondylus* (STREP-toe-SPON-dih-lus) may never be fully understood because important specimens of them were lost in this way—a sort of second extinction.

Q. Which Mesozoic dinosaur had a lot of guts?

A. When *Scipionyx* (sip-pee-AH-nicks) was named in 1998, it was the first fossil dinosaur skeleton to be found in Italy. The animal, which died very shortly after hatching, was preserved in a way that shows some of its soft anatomy. The soft parts of animals almost never survive fossilization, so a rare find like this is very important. The nine-inch fossil of *Scipionyx* was found with its muscles, liver, and intestines all visible. For such a little youngster, *Scipionyx* sure had a lot of guts!

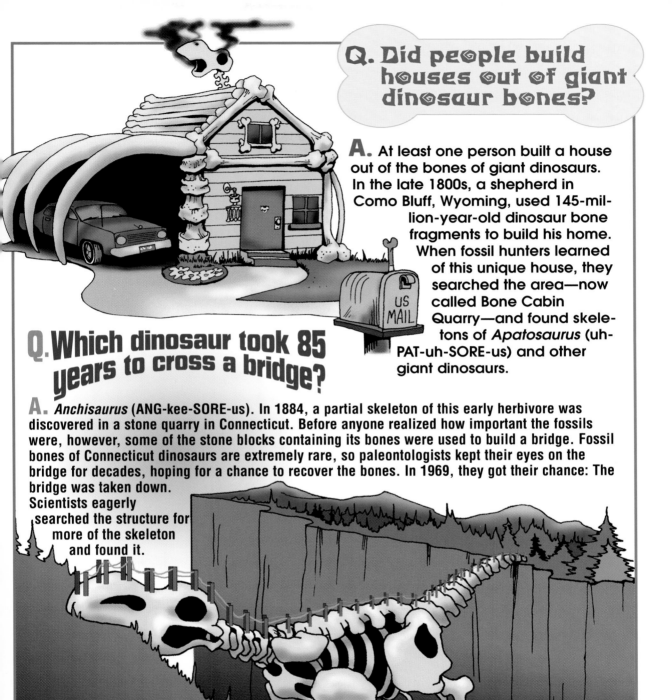

Q. Did people build houses out of giant dinosaur bones?

A. At least one person built a house out of the bones of giant dinosaurs. In the late 1800s, a shepherd in Como Bluff, Wyoming, used 145-million-year-old dinosaur bone fragments to build his home. When fossil hunters learned of this unique house, they searched the area—now called Bone Cabin Quarry—and found skeletons of *Apatosaurus* (uh-PAT-uh-SORE-us) and other giant dinosaurs.

Q. Which dinosaur took 85 years to cross a bridge?

A. *Anchisaurus* (ANG-kee-SORE-us). In 1884, a partial skeleton of this early herbivore was discovered in a stone quarry in Connecticut. Before anyone realized how important the fossils were, however, some of the stone blocks containing its bones were used to build a bridge. Fossil bones of Connecticut dinosaurs are extremely rare, so paleontologists kept their eyes on the bridge for decades, hoping for a chance to recover the bones. In 1969, they got their chance: The bridge was taken down. Scientists eagerly searched the structure for more of the skeleton and found it.

Q. DID DINOSAURS HAVE BLACK BONES WHEN THEY WERE ALIVE?

A. No. The bones of dinosaur skeletons in museums are sometimes black. However, dinosaur bones were originally white, just like the bones of animals living today. Over time, bones that are buried underground pick up different colors. Water flowing through the ground carries minerals that can get inside buried bones and stay there. Fossil bones can become black, brown, red, yellow, green, or blue, depending on the minerals left there. The color of a fossilized bone is determined by the minerals present, not the bone's age.

Q. Did Cretaceous dinosaurs think that insects were boring?

A. Boring as in dull, no; boring as in making holes, yes! Mongolia is a great place to find complete, well-preserved dinosaur fossils. Sometimes, however, they have been found with round holes drilled through the bones. What happened? The holes were made by insect larvae that hatched from eggs buried with the dead animal. After the insects hatched and ate their fill of the dinosaur's carcass, they bored up through the skeleton to reach the surface. That left tunnels in the bones through which they burrowed.

Q. Which dinosaurs served us green eggs and ham?

A. You could say that titanosaurs (ty-**TAN**-uh-sorz) have. In November 1997, a huge dinosaur nesting ground was discovered in Patagonia, Argentina. The ground was littered with the greenish fragments of thousands of fossil eggs from titanosaurs, which were huge, long-necked herbivores. Many eggs were collected from this site, including some with tiny bones and even skin impressions of unhatched titanosaurs. To transport the excavated egg clusters, the diggers wrapped them in plaster to protect them from damage. These plaster jackets were nicknamed "hams," because that is what they looked like.

Q. What are "spoonbill" dinosaurs?

A. Back in the 1880s, a scientist named Edward Drinker Cope was describing the fossil dinosaur that we now call *Anatotitan* (uh-NAT-uh-TY-tan). *Anatotitan* was a giant herbivore that lived 65 million years ago. Cope noticed that this dinosaur's beak looked very similar to that of a modern bird called the spoonbill. For a while, dinosaurs with this kind of beak were called spoonbill dinosaurs. Then, in 1901, the American Museum of Natural History published a story about Barnum Brown, a famous fossil hunter. The story used the word *duckbill* to describe spoonbill dinosaurs. That label stuck, and duckbill is the name that we use today.

Q. Did dinosaurs ever build dams?

A. No, but some of them *became* dams. When dinosaurs died, their bodies sometimes wound up in rivers or streams. These gigantic carcasses often blocked the flow of water, as well as anything flowing downstream. The bodies of other, smaller animals were often buried with these colossal skeletons. One plant-eating dinosaur found in Wyoming was preserved with fish, tiny dinosaurs, mammals, frogs, turtles, crocodiles, and flying reptiles that had been trapped against its enormous body! The body also collected mud and sand, which eventually buried and preserved the entire fossil zoo.

Q. HOW BiG WAS THE BiGGEST DiNOSAUR POOP?

A. Some sauropods were over 150 feet long and weighed as much as 150 cows. If a cow poops 2 1/2 pounds every day, just imagine how much a gigantic sauropod would poop! The result would be bigger and heavier than you. Fossilized poops—called coprolites—tell us a lot about extinct animals. Sauropod coprolites show the broken bits of plants that these giants ate. The biggest dinosaurs clearly ate *their* veggies!

Q. What was the biggest dinosaur (egg) ever found?

A. The largest eggs from a Mesozoic dinosaur were cantaloupe-sized. They came from the giant plant-eating titanosaurs that sometimes reached lengths of more than 100 feet. But the largest eggs ever, strange as it may sound, are from a bird! The extinct moa, *Aepyornis maximus* (AY-pee-OR-nis MAX-ih-mus) laid eggs as big as watermelons.

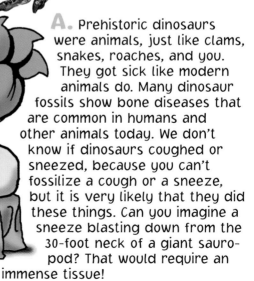

Q. Did dinosaurs ever get sick?

A. Prehistoric dinosaurs were animals, just like clams, snakes, roaches, and you. They got sick like modern animals do. Many dinosaur fossils show bone diseases that are common in humans and other animals today. We don't know if dinosaurs coughed or sneezed, because you can't fossilize a cough or a sneeze, but it is very likely that they did these things. Can you imagine a sneeze blasting down from the 30-foot neck of a giant sauropod? That would require an immense tissue!

Q.
Which well-known dinosaur was once called *Hypsirophus*?

A. The dinosaur *Hypsirophus* (hip-suh-ROH-fus) *(near right)* was named in 1878 for its tall vertebrae (backbones). The name means "high-roofed." At first, scientists thought that it was a large carnivorous dinosaur, because the teeth of a meat-eater were found with its bones. However, when bones of *Hypsirophus* were compared with bones of the plant-eating *Stegosaurus*, scientists realized that they were the same kind of animal. *Stegosaurus* was named first, in 1877, so its name was kept. As for the sharp teeth, they turned out to belong to an *Allosaurus (far right)* that probably had been feeding on the *Stegosaurus*.

Q. DID A DINOSAUR EVER ATTACK FRANCE?

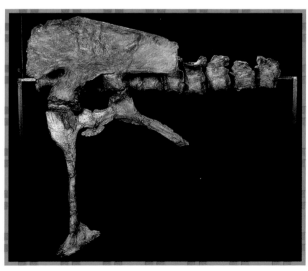

A. Well, not exactly. Fossil bones of a carnivorous dinosaur were found recently near the town of Tarascon, in southern France. According to local legend, a dragonlike monster called the *Tarasque* once tormented the people of this town. So, in 1991, the dinosaur found nearby was given the name *Tarascosaurus* (tuh-RAS-kuh-SORE-us), which means "Tarasque lizard." *Tarascosaurus* couldn't have been the dragon that frightened the people of Tarascon—giant dinosaurs were extinct long before people lived in France. Maybe the people of Tarascon had seen dinosaur bones, such as the hip bone at left, and created a dragon myth based on them.

Q. Did dinosaurs ever wear j e w e l r y ?

A. Of course not! However, a dinosaur could *become* jewelry—or at least a kind of gemstone. Jewel-like dinosaur fossils have been found in Grawin, New South Wales, Australia. Fossil bones are sometimes preserved as chunks of opal, a semiprecious stone. Recently, the toe bone of a carnivorous dinosaur was found preserved as opal; the exact shape of the bone remained in the form of a dazzling gem. Imagine a complete fossilized skeleton of a dinosaur made out of brilliant opal! Keep your eyes open—it might be out there.

Q. Which meat-eating dinosaur could be called cool, calm, and collected?

A. Of the very few known prehistoric Antarctic dinosaurs, the meat-eating *Cryolophosaurus* (KRY-uh-loaf-uh-SORE-us) was definitely cool, calm, and collected. Any dinosaur from the frozen Antarctic would be "cool," but *Cryolophosaurus (left)* was also cool because it had a crazy-looking crest on its head. It was "calm" because it was buried for 193 million years—a silence long enough to calm anyone! When it was "collected" in 1994, it became the first ancient Antarctic dinosaur to be named.

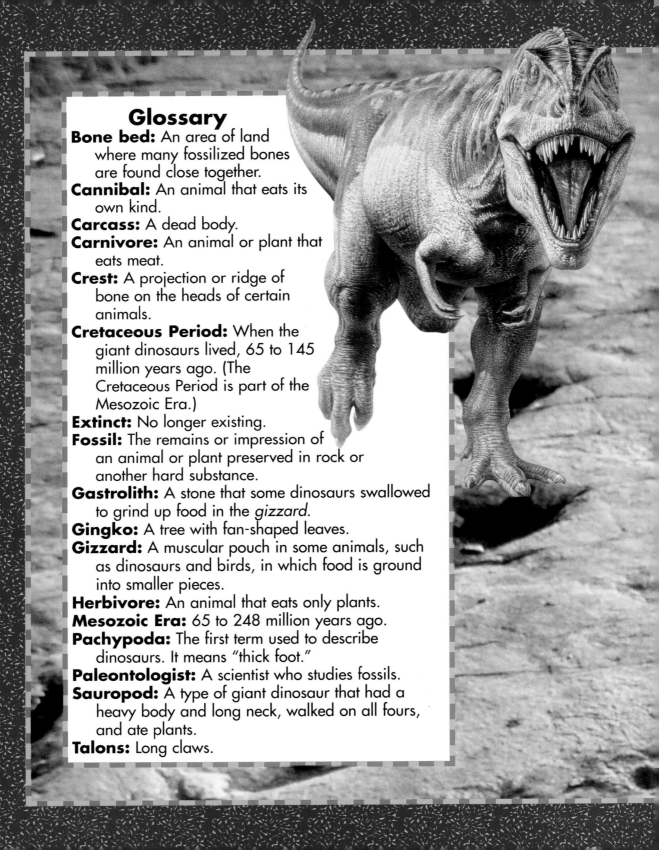

Glossary

Bone bed: An area of land where many fossilized bones are found close together.

Cannibal: An animal that eats its own kind.

Carcass: A dead body.

Carnivore: An animal or plant that eats meat.

Crest: A projection or ridge of bone on the heads of certain animals.

Cretaceous Period: When the giant dinosaurs lived, 65 to 145 million years ago. (The Cretaceous Period is part of the Mesozoic Era.)

Extinct: No longer existing.

Fossil: The remains or impression of an animal or plant preserved in rock or another hard substance.

Gastrolith: A stone that some dinosaurs swallowed to grind up food in the *gizzard*.

Gingko: A tree with fan-shaped leaves.

Gizzard: A muscular pouch in some animals, such as dinosaurs and birds, in which food is ground into smaller pieces.

Herbivore: An animal that eats only plants.

Mesozoic Era: 65 to 248 million years ago.

Pachypoda: The first term used to describe dinosaurs. It means "thick foot."

Paleontologist: A scientist who studies fossils.

Sauropod: A type of giant dinosaur that had a heavy body and long neck, walked on all fours, and ate plants.

Talons: Long claws.